An Irish Blessing
for the Home

An Irish Blessing for the Home

for the Home

WELLERAN POLTARNEES

LAUGHING ELEPHANT BOOKS   MMII

ISBN 1-883211-50-6

FIRST PRINTING ALL RIGHTS RESERVED
PRINTED IN SINGAPORE

LAUGHING ELEPHANT BOOKS
3645 INTERLAKE AVENUE NORTH
SEATTLE WASHINGTON 98103

God bless the corners of this house,

and be the lintel blessed.

Bless the hearth,

the table too,

and bless each place of rest.

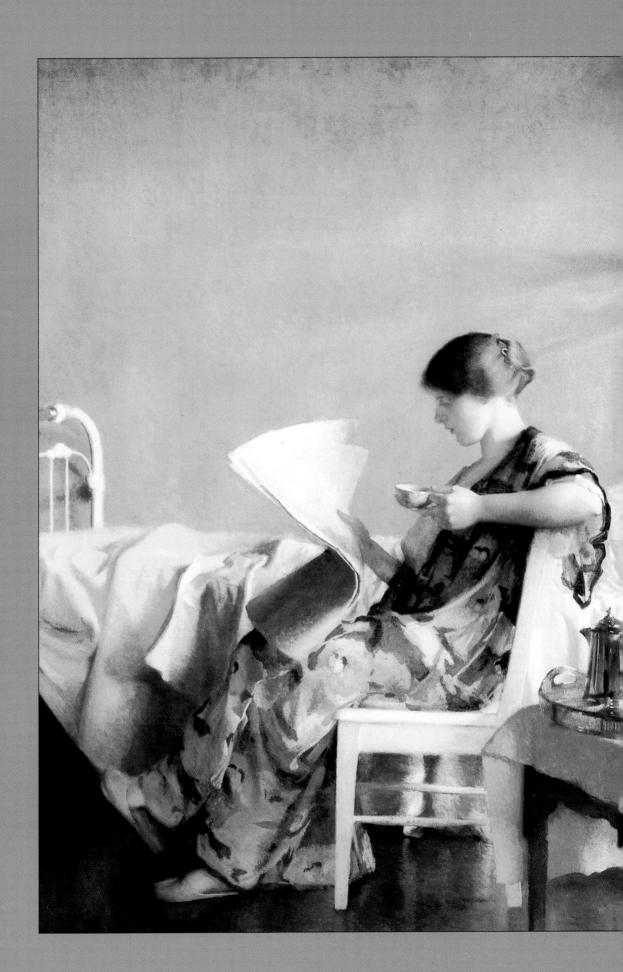

Bless each door that opens wide

to stranger,

kith and kin;

Bless each shining window-pane

that lets the sunshine in.

Bless the roof-tree up above.

Bless every solid wall.

The peace of man,

the peace of love,

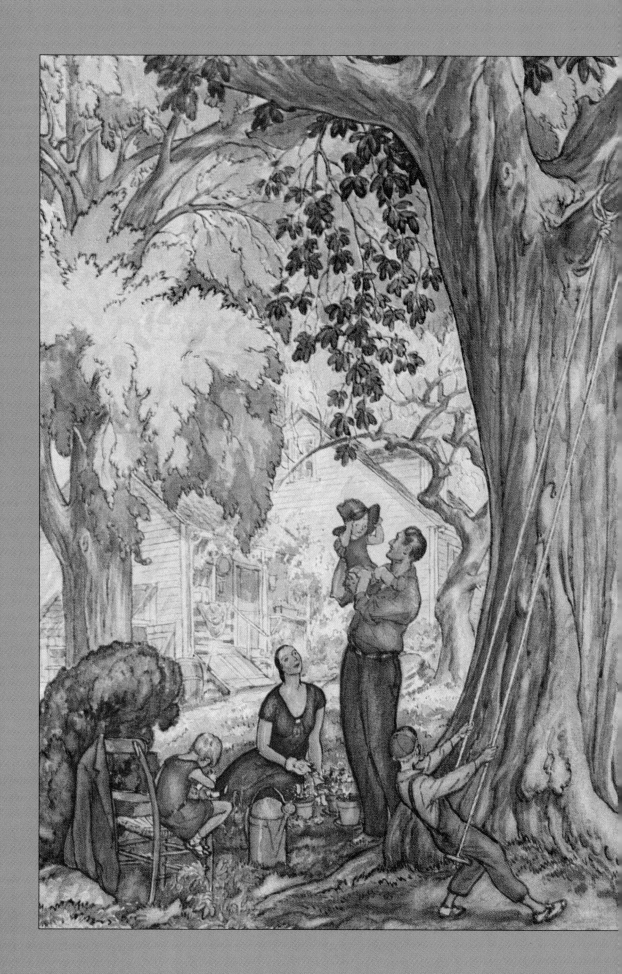

the peace of God on all.

Picture Credits

Cover   Maurice Day. Magazine cover, 1920.

Endpapers   Anonymous, n.d.

Half Title   Anonymous Magazine Cover, 1925.

Frontispiece   Henri Le Sidaner. "Table dans la Verdure," 1926.

Title Page   Paul Keller Reutlingen. "Watching the Geese," n.d.

Copyright   Florence McAnelly. From *Winter Is Here*, 1955.

Page 2   Dennis Miller Bunker. "Roadside Cottage," 1889.

Page 3   Ethel M. Found, c. 1920.

Page 4   Abbott Fuller Graves. "Kennebunk Door," n.d.

Page 5   Henri Martin. "La Porte D'Entrée à Marquairol," n.d.

Page 6   Anonymous Magazine Cover, 1933.

Page 7   Henry Grinnell Thompson, "Early Twilight," c. 1918.

Page 8   Henri Le Sidaner. "La Table aux Lanternes," 1924.

Page 9   Fanny Brate. "Nameday," 1902.

Page 10   Henri Lebasque. "La Sieste," 1923.

Page 11   William McGregor Paxton. "The Morning Paper," 1913.

Page 12   C.K. Magazine Illustration, 1936.

Page 13   Prins Eugen. "Afton, Lilla Tyresö," 1905.

Page 14   Florence and Margaret Hoopes and Margaret Freeman.
     From *Childhood Readers: Good Friends – A Primer*, 1932.

Page 15   Gotthardt Kuehl. "Das Gartenzimmer," c. 1890.

Page 16   Anonymous advertisement, 1913.

Page 17   Carl Larsson. "Kersti På Skoleophold I Falun," 1910.

Page 18   Childe Hassam. "The Goldfish Window," 1916.

Picture Credits

Page 19   Mildred Anne Butler. "A Window at Kilmurray," n.d.

Page 20   Moritz von Schwind. "The Morning Hour," 1858.

Page 21   Henri Le Sidaner. "Intimité Rose et Or," 1930.

Page 22   Anonymous Magazine Illustration, 1926.

Page 23   Anonymous Magazine Cover, 1940.

Page 24   George Bellows. "My House, Woodstock," 1924.

Page 25   Atkinson Grimshaw.

"Autumn Glory: The Old Mill, Cheshire," 1869.

Page 26   Stanislaw Julianovich Zukowski. "Terrace," 1906.

Page 27   Frederick Carl Frieseke. "Blue Girl Reading," 1935.

Page 28   Henri Lebasque. "La Terrasse," 1913.

Page 29   Anonymous Magazine Illustration, 1932.

Page 30   Jean-François Millet. "Spring," c. 1870.

Page 31   Florence Harrison. From *Elfin Song*, 1912.

Back Cover   Childe Hassam. "Moonlight, The Old House," 1906.

Designed at Blue Lantern Studio
by Mike Harrison and Sacheverell Darling

Typeset in Didot